LEPAGE'S
TOY-CRAFT
BOOK

with

*full directions
for making
twenty-five
fascinating toys*

with

LEPAGE'S GLUE

Published by
RUSSIA CEMENT COMPANY
Gloucester, Mass.

Copyright April, 1925, by
RUSSIA CEMENT COMPANY
Gloucester, Mass.

A List of the Toys Described

You can have endless fun with this new way to make your own toys

WHAT do you do on stormy days? Wouldn't it be wonderful if a magical sack, as big as you are, suddenly appeared before you, bulging with all manner of fascinating toys that began to tumble out of it at your feet! Would you care whether it were raining? I should say not! That would be one of the finest days you ever spent.

LePage's Toy-Craft Book is just like that magical sack. It is crammed full of directions for making fascinating toys that you can make yourself—bridges, windmills, submarines, racing automobiles, lighthouses, airplanes, castles, toy furniture, and many other things.

Glance through the index on the opposite page and see the list of toys you can make. You can make small villages or towns if you wish with houses, churches, office buildings, and automobiles in the streets. If you use your imagination, the actual toys described in this book are by no means all that you can make. Having made these toys you will get the knack of Toy-Craft and be able to make many other fascinating things that your imagination will suggest to you.

Some boys like to make theatres. If your tastes are inclined towards things theatrical, you will no doubt be able, after you have had some experience and practice in LePage's Toy-Craft, to make a stage with footlights, curtains, scenery, furniture. You can cut out illustrations of people and lepage them on heavy cardboard so that they can be the actors and actresses on your stage. You can probably find pictures of your favorite moving picture stars and make them act for you.

If you have an electric railway, you will be able to make additional equipment like semaphores, bridges, tunnels and stations. Yes, bridges strong enough for your train to run across in perfect safety.

Many of the things that this book describes will be of as much interest to girls as to boys. Doll's house furniture is especially included for girls.

These suggestions are only a foretaste of what you can make and the fun you can have.

And all you need is this LePage's Toy-Craft Book, LePage's Glue, a ruler, a pencil, some cardboard and a pair of scissors.

LePage's Toy-Craft is something that will grow on you. You will like it better and better the more toys you make. And before you know it, out of odds and ends of material that cost nothing, you will be making toys that your family will think a marvelous accomplishment on your part, and that you will be immensely proud to show your friends.

Read the general directions carefully on the following pages, and then you are all set for some toy-making fun. Just follow the directions and diagrams carefully, and you will be surprised and delighted at your own amazing skillfulness.

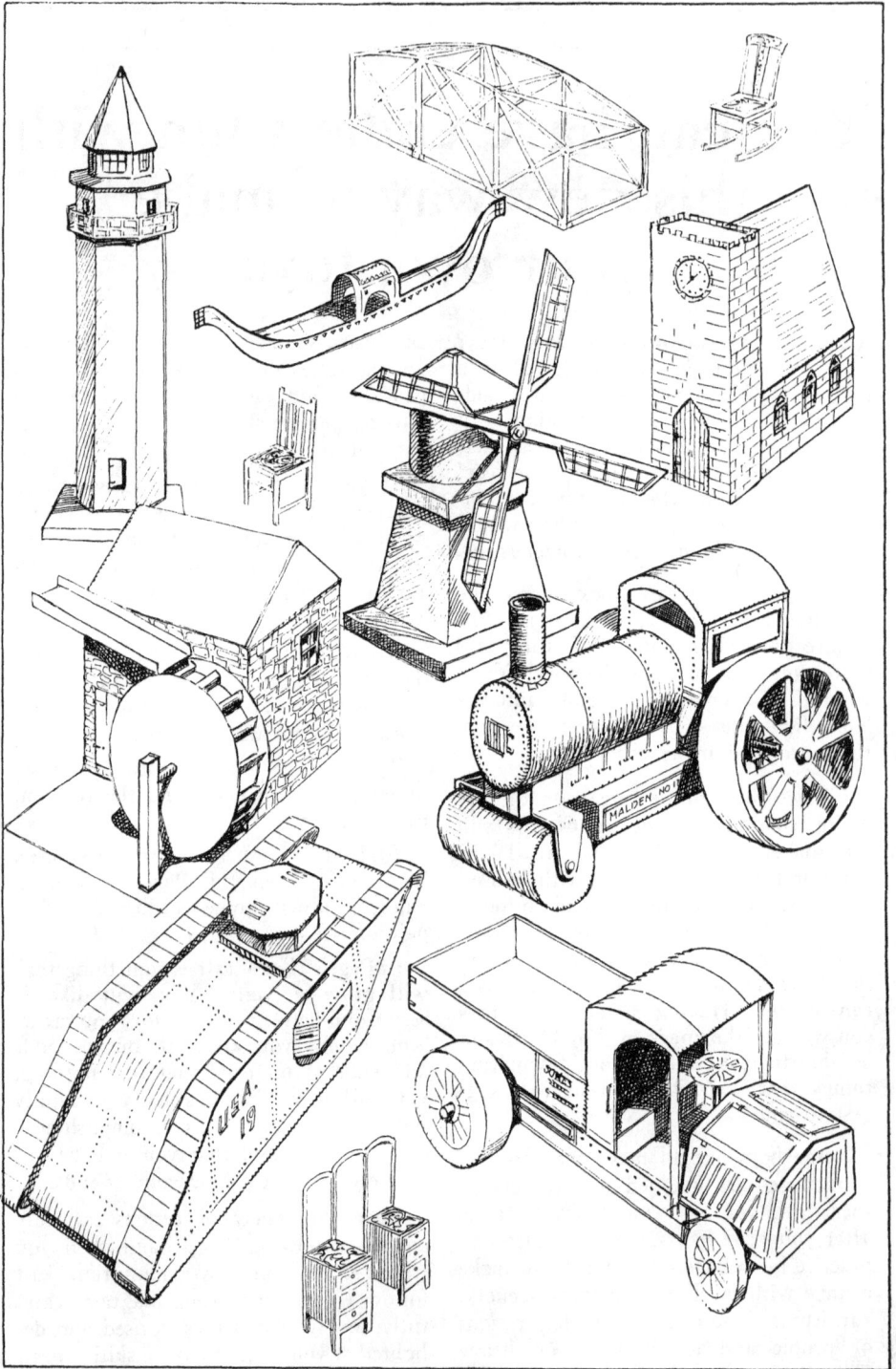

Above are illustrated a few of the toys made by following
the directions given in this book

General Directions for the use of LePage's Glue in Toy-Craft

EVERY toy described in this book can be made with LePage's Glue. This powerful adhesive will, therefore, be your most important tool. Just as in carpentering you would use hammer, plane and saw, in Toy-Craft you use LePage's Glue. And just as you would learn how to handle a plane or saw, you should learn how to handle LePage's Glue.

Before beginning your first toy, it will be best to practice using LePage's a little on scraps of paper and cardboard. As a general rule be careful not to use too much. Remove the stopper (which is also the spreader) from the tube. Gently squeeze the bottom of the tube so that a little glue is forced out onto the paper or cardboard. Spread it evenly over the surface with the spreader. Let it become almost dry and then press another piece of cardboard on top of it. You will find that they stick quickly, securely and without slipping. If you use too much glue, or if you do not wait for the glue to become almost dry before placing the second piece of cardboard over it, the surfaces will not stick together so quickly.

If you wish to make an extra strong joint, spread LePage's over both surfaces instead of over only one, and then let it become almost dry before placing them together.

In using LePage's on wood, you proceed as with cardboard, only you may have to use a little more glue. If the wood is very soft, like soft pine, let the first coat of glue become thoroughly dry. Then apply a second coat, let this become almost dry, and then place the surfaces together. Joints made in this way will hold forever.

When the surfaces to be joined are large, squeeze the glue directly onto the surface as above, but use a small piece of cardboard to spread it around with. This will be quicker for large surfaces than using the metal spreader which comes with the tube.

It is convenient to keep two cloths handy; one damp and one dry. If your fingers become sticky, moisten them with the damp cloth to take off the glue, and dry them with the dry cloth.

Hereafter in this book, when we speak of glue we will always say "LePage's"; for everyone knows that "LePage's" is the name of the very finest glue made. And whenever we wish to say, "Now glue these surfaces together," we will say instead, "Now lepage these surfaces together." Those are the words which every skillful Toy-Craft worker uses.

FIG. A

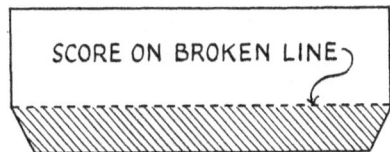

SCORE ON BROKEN LINE

General Directions A — "How to make a flange." There are two methods of joining edges of cardboard together: by means of a flange and by means of a hinge. A flange is an extra bit of cardboard left attached to one edge when the cardboard shape is cut out. Figure "A" illustrates a flange. In the diagrams which follow in the book, a flange is always indicated by cross-rule shading. Score along the broken line by creasing with a blunt point, like the point of a pair of scissors. Then you can bend the flange and lepage it to the other edge of cardboard. Whenever the edges to be joined are to be bent in a curve, as in making a wheel, the flange should be cut like the teeth of a saw. See Figure "B." The sharper the curve, the finer the teeth. Score and bend the flange before cutting the teeth in the flange. This is much easier than trying to score and bend each tooth separately.

FIG. B

SCORE ON BROKEN LINE

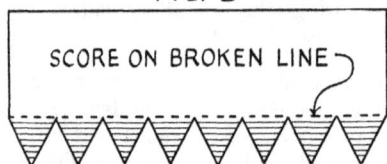

General Directions B—"How to make a hinge." In some cases it is easier to make a hinge than it is to leave a flange. A hinge is simply a strip of paper or cardboard which is lepaged in place so that it straddles the joint. Score or fold the strip down the center. Then each side becomes a flange. One flange is lepaged to one of the two edges to be joined, and the other flange is lepaged to the other edge. See Figure "C."

FIG. C HINGE

SCORE ON BROKEN LINE

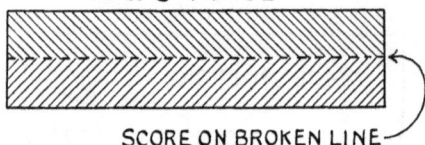

The simplest toys are described at the beginning of the book. We advise starting with the easiest ones.

You will need to know that the radius of a circle is the distance from its center to any point on its edge or circumference. Its diameter is twice as long as its radius.

The qualities of LePage's that make it easy and practical to use

LePage's is pure. Owing to its purity it will not weaken or soften and lose its hold upon exposure to dampness. A good joint will always remain good under the most trying conditions.

LePage's has tremendous holding power. You will be interested to know of a test that was made a few years ago, successfully demonstrating the wonderful strength of LePage's.

A piece of oak one inch square was sawed in two diagonally and then put together again with LePage's taken from one of the regular bottles. Then from this lepaged joint a Ford automobile was suspended from a framework erected on the platform of a five-ton truck. And two men, sitting in the Ford, rode the entire length of a Fourth-of-July Parade. The entire weight of the Ford and the two men was held up by the lepaged joint. And it was raining all the time. If the tiny joint had parted, men and auto would have had a tumble, but LePage's stood the strain.

LePage's is carefully preserved by secret processes. It will keep in its proper condition in any climate.

LePage's dries with a tough (hard) elastic film. It does not become brittle and crumble and powder off as pastes and other adhesives have a tendency to do.

Materials for making toys

ONE of the most desirable features of LePage's Toy-Craft, is the idea of using almost useless waste materials for the making of these practical, and delightful toys. There is usually no need for you to purchase cardboard or paper to make these toys. Old suit-boxes, hat boxes, candy boxes and the like, will serve admirably in furnishing you with all the materials necessary for the construction of the toys included in this booklet.

To enable the young toy-maker to work with speed and accuracy, the Russia Cement Company has prepared a special set of instruments, known as the LePage's Craft Kit. This valuable kit may be bought at stores, or by sending the regular price of $2.00 to the Russia

Cement Company, Gloucester, Mass. LePage's Glue may be bought at drug, hardware, department and stationery stores. If there is anything you need for Toy-Craft which you cannot buy at home, write a letter to us about it, addressing The Editor, LePage's Craft League, Gloucester, Mass.

Explanation of diagrams

WHEREVER you see a solid line, it means you are to cut along that line. Wherever you see a broken line, it means you are to score with a knife or scissors and fold. Wherever you see a shaded portion it represents a flange and means that you are to lepage this section to some other section. Dimensions are given in inches and fractions of inches. A piece of cardboard three and one-half inches long by two inches wide is given as: a piece of cardboard 3½" x 2".

The diagram below shows how solid lines, broken lines and flanges are indicated in the diagrams for making the toys. Follow them carefully.

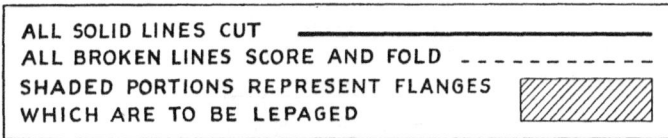

```
ALL SOLID LINES CUT ————————
ALL BROKEN LINES SCORE AND FOLD - - - - - - - -
SHADED PORTIONS REPRESENT FLANGES
WHICH ARE TO BE LEPAGED
```

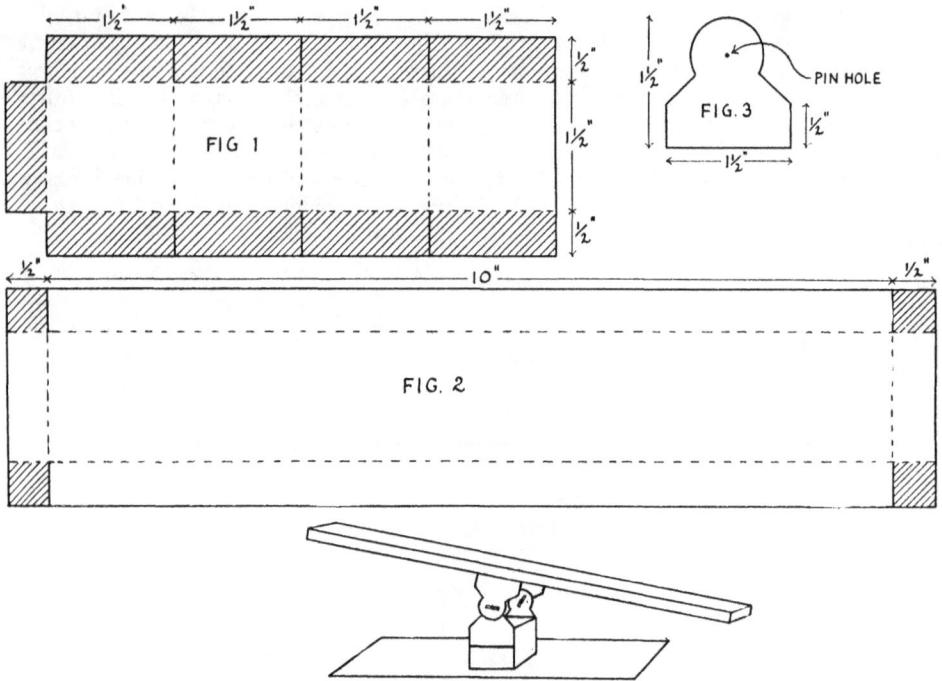

How to make a Teeter Board

CUT a piece of cardboard 8 inches x 3 inches for the base on which the teeter board is built. Cut a second piece of cardboard, using Fig. 1 as a pattern. This folds into a cubical box open at two sides. Lepage the flanges which surround one of these open sides to the exact center of the 8 x 3 inch base. Cut a piece of cardboard 1½ inches square and lepage over the remaining open end of the cubical box. Now cut out four brackets, using Fig. 3 for a pattern for each. The round top of the bracket is obtained by tracing part way around a penny. Make a pin hole in the center of the round part of each of these four brackets. Cut a piece of cardboard using Fig. 2 as a pattern. Fold this, lepaging the flanges inside the long edges. In the exact center of each of the long sides lepage a bracket, round part down. Lepage a bracket, round part up, to the sides of the cubical box. Bring the four brackets together. They will match in pairs. Stick a pin through the pin holes of each pair.

How to make a Canoe

CUT a piece of cardboard 6½ inches x 2½ inches. See Fig. 4. Score down the center lengthwise, dividing the cardboard into halves. On one half draw the shape of the side of the canoe, using a silver half dollar to get the proper curves at the ends. Cut along the outline of this half. Fold along the scored line. Trace the outline of the first half on the second half. Cut along the outline of the second half. Lepage the curved edges together. Now cut a seat, Fig. 5, and lepage in the center between the sides of the canoe. You will be

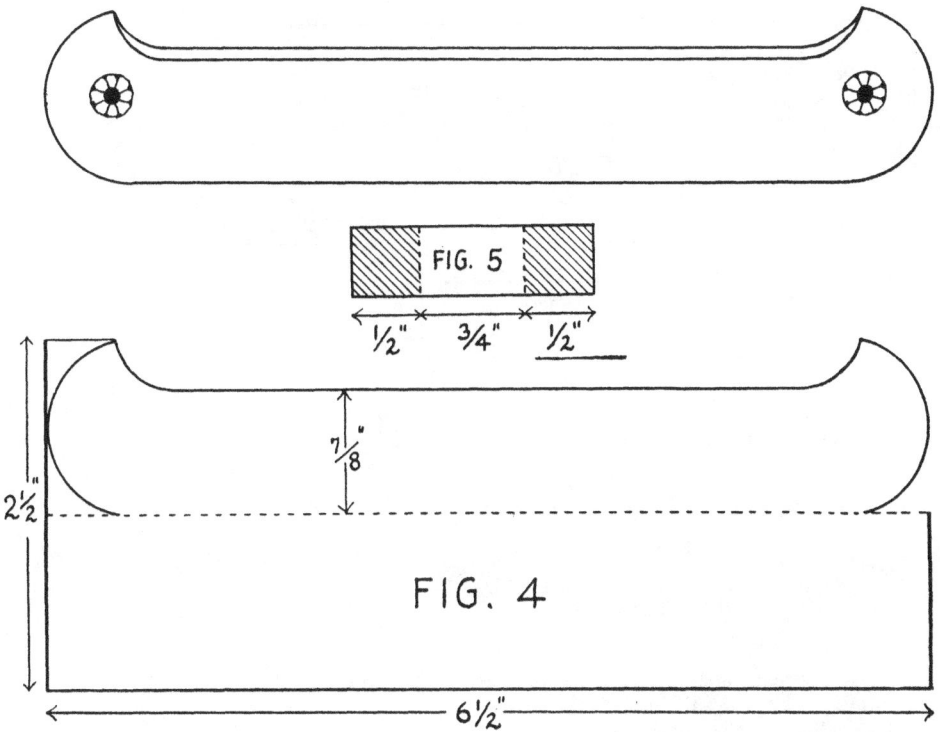

FIG. 5

½" ¾" ½"

7⅛"

2½"

FIG. 4

6½"

pleased with its gracefulness, and with a little experimenting you can make a much larger one. Some consider them-selves lucky to have a piece of birch bark to work with instead of cardboard. Then they have a real Indian canoe.

How to make a Venetian Gondola

THE gondola is made of five pieces of cardboard: two sides, bottom, deck and awning. First cut out the sides. See Fig. 6. Here we have a piece of cardboard 9" x 2½" overall. On line AA indicate with a pencil dot a po-sition 2½" from each end. Draw line BB 1¼" above line AA and parallel to AA. On line BB indicate with a pencil dot a position 1½" from each end. Make pencil dots also ½" from corners, CC. These dots are a guide for drawing the curves. Now draw the curves in free hand on one end, tracing the outline for the other end. Now cut out and make another side just like this first one. Lepage these two sides to-gether at bow and stern by spreading LePage's over the surfaces between the ends and lines drawn between points B and D and then placing together. Now you are ready for the bottom and the deck.

Cut a piece of cardboard 6" x 2". See Fig. 7. Follow dimensions shown and cut along line EE. Then cut a saw tooth flange around and you will have a shape like Fig. 8. Make a duplicate of this for the deck. The curve of the dotted line is drawn free hand. With the lines of Fig. 7 to guide you this will be easy. Score along this dotted line and bend the teeth all over in the same direction.

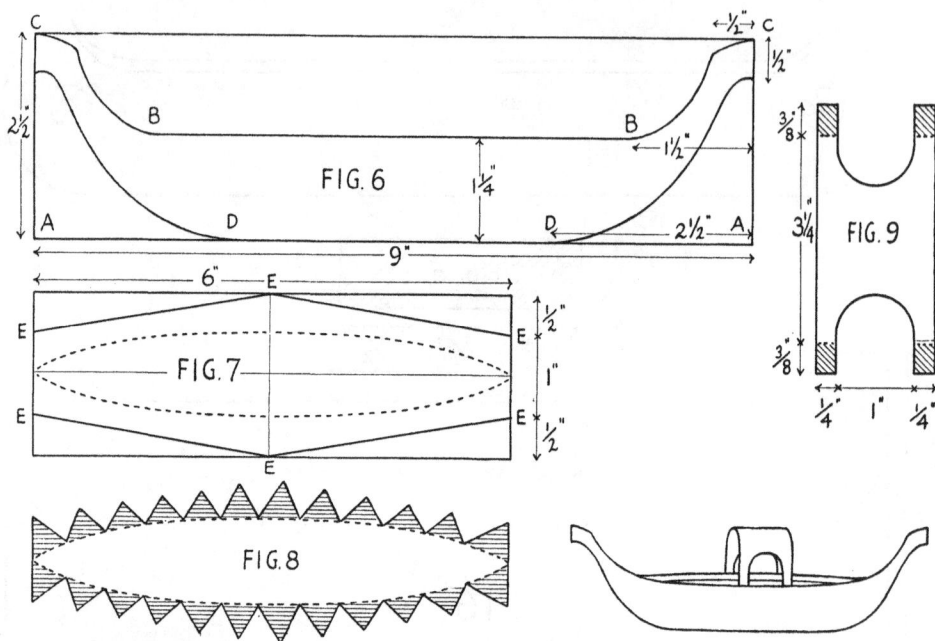

FIG. 6

FIG. 7

FIG. 8

FIG. 9

Now spread apart the sides of the gondola. Lepage all along the inside lower edges of the sides. Insert one of the shapes like Fig. 8 through the top, teeth pointing up. Push to bottom and press into place. Now lepage the deck close to the top edge of the sides, putting the teeth downward this time. If some parts get down too far, pick them up with a pin.

Then cut a piece of cardboard 3¼″ x 1½″. Leave flanges ½″ square at the four corners. The curves are made by tracing around a nickel. This forms the awning. Bend the flanges in and lepage them to the deck, and your gondola is complete.

How to make a Viking Dragon Ship of the 9th Century

THE two sides are made exactly as you made the sides of the gondola, following Fig. 6. Only two things are different. One is the curve at each end. One is to represent the head and one the tail, as if the ship were a loathsome dragon leaping over the waves. The other difference is that along the line BB, see Fig. 6, you draw circles by tracing around a dime, to represent the shields made of hides which the Vikings used. The bottom and deck are made exactly like Figs. 7 and 8 for the gon-dola and lepaged in place in the same way. Punch a hole through the deck for the stem of the mast, a little nearer the head than the tail. The hole is large enough for your pencil to slip in loosely.

Instead of an awning, you can now erect a mast and spread a sail. Cut a strip of paper 5 inches wide and long enough so that when rolled up tightly it forms a mast as big around as a pencil. Lepage the edge in place. Then place a thick drop of LePage's on one

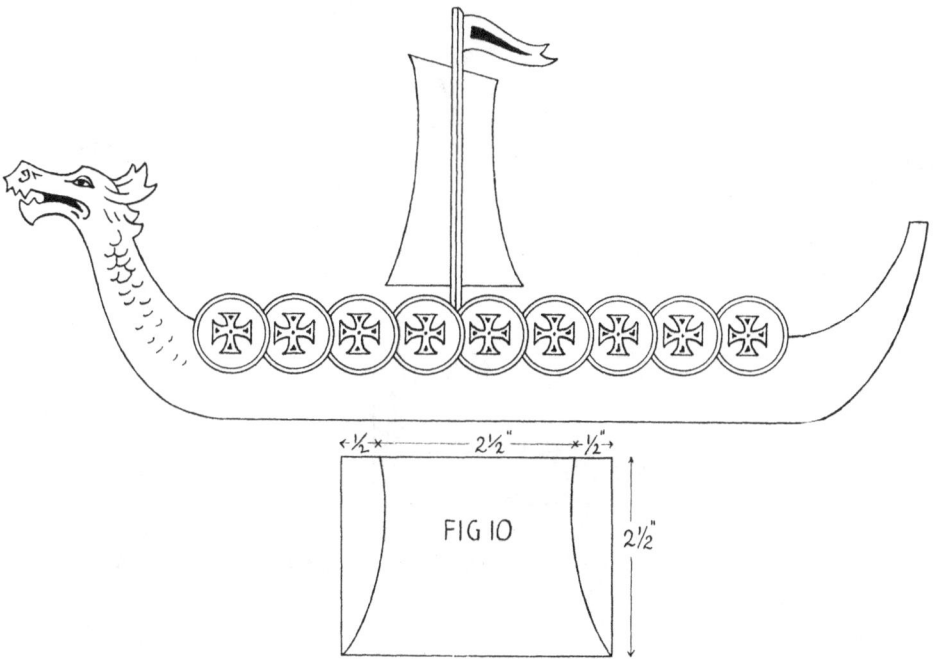

FIG 10

end and push down through the hole in the deck until it is firmly on the bottom. Now cut out the sail following Fig. 10. Lepage to the mast, leaving room at the top for a flag. If you are a good hand with crayons or water colors, you can now paint this handsome ship.

How to make a Bird House

CUT a piece of cardboard 11" x 4" and, following dimensions carefully, draw on it the lines shown in Fig. 11. Cut all solid lines. Score all broken lines. You will see how this folds up so that the flange at the extreme left of Fig. 11 is lepaged inside the edge of the house at the extreme right of Fig. 11. Cut a piece of cardboard 3" x 2" and lepage this to the flanges that fold in at the bottom of the house.

Cut a piece of cardboard 5" x 3½" and score as shown in Fig. 12. This is the roof. It is large enough to allow for gables and eaves. Bend in the flanges along the gables and along the tops of the sides. Apply LePage's to them. Fasten the roof in place. Cut a piece of cardboard 8½" x 4½" as shown in Fig. 13. This folds up and is lepaged into a square column for the upright support. Lepage the top of this column to the center of the bottom of the house. Lepage the bottom of this column to the center of a piece of cardboard 4" x 4". Now you are all ready for the birds. Even a tiny porch is provided for them to land on.

Later you will find it an interesting experiment to make a more elaborate house. If you have a copy of House Beautiful or House and Garden or any other magazine that shows pictures of houses, you can select one that pleases you and work out a pattern for it, following Fig. 11 as the general scheme.

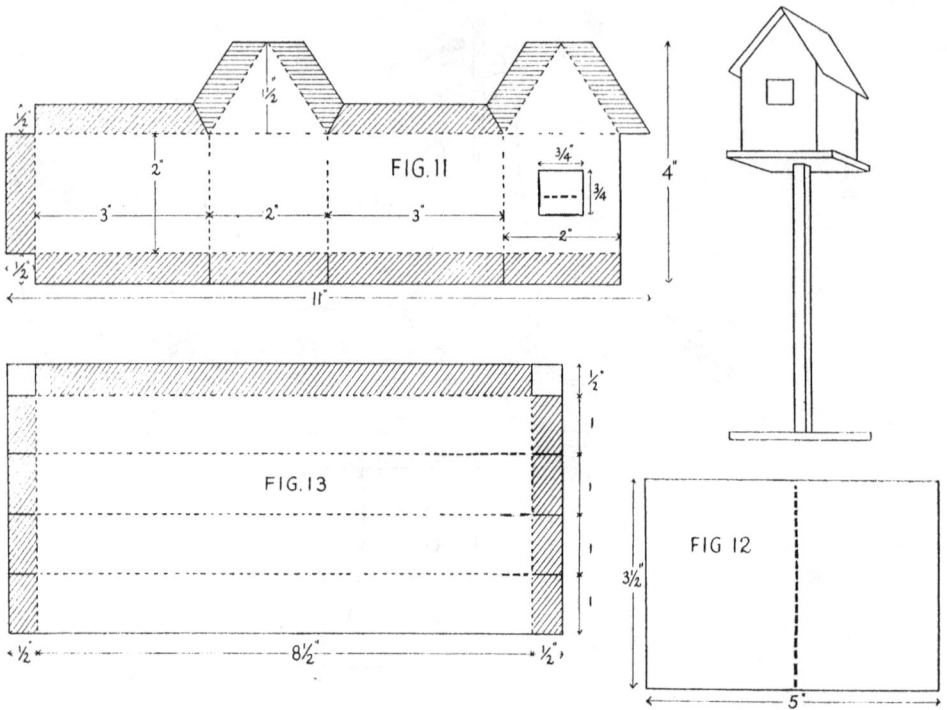

FIG. 11

FIG. 13

FIG 12

How to make a Doll's Hammock Swing

FOR the base on which the swing rests cut a piece of heavy cardboard 12″ x 5″. Three inches from the ends draw lines across this cardboard to indicate the position of the upright supports. Cut out the two upright supports, following Fig. 14. Heavy cardboard should be used. If only light cardboard is available, make more than two shapes and lepage together. Score along broken line for flange at bottom and lepage this flange to the base along the pencil lines you drew as directed above.

Cut a piece of cardboard 7″ x 2″. Score a ½″ flange at each end. Make pin holes as indicated in Fig. 15, through which the ropes will be slung. Bend the flanges downward and lepage to the inner edges of the two upright supports. Cut a piece of cardboard 9″ x 6½″ and draw lines on it, following Fig. 16 accurately. The four heavy dots on the main section are pin holes for the ropes. Fig. 16 folds up into the swing itself. Lepage all flanges in place. Hang the swing in place with string through the corresponding pin holes. Lepage strips of cardboard ½″ wide with ½″ flanges at each end, from the four corners of the base to the four corners of the top to give necessary rigidity.

How to make a Church

CUT a piece of cardboard 22½″ x 7″. Score it and cut it out according to Fig. 17. Fold up and lepage flange at extreme left to inside of edge at ex-

treme right. This is the main body of the church. For the rear end, trace the outline on a sheet of cardboard, cut out and lepage to the flanges provided.

FIG. 16

FIG 14

FIG. 15

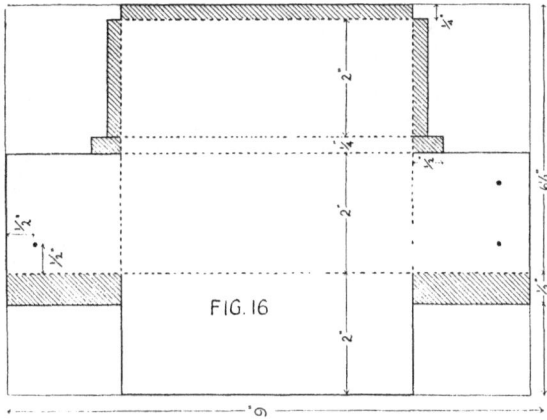

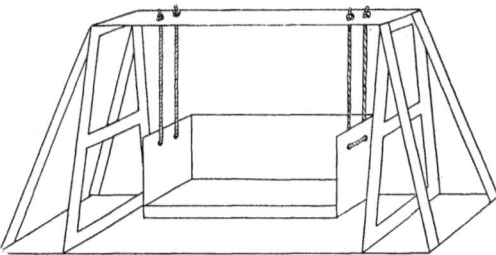

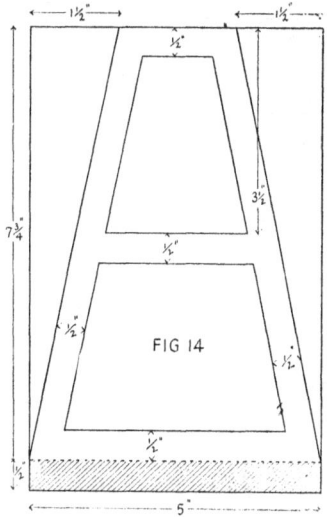

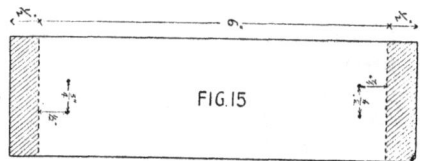

Cut a piece of cardboard 13½" x 10" and score according to Fig. 18. Fold up and lepage flange at extreme left to inside of edge at extreme right. Cut two pieces of cardboard, each 4½" x 2" and lepage one to the top and one to the bottom of this tower.

Cover the flanges at the open front end of the main body of the church with LePage's and fasten to the tower. This finishes the building of the church. Now you have an opportunity to decorate it, drawing windows; stones for the walls; shingles for the roof.

Having made this very simple church, you may become ambitious to have a number of different types of churches, representing different styles of architecture or typical of different religions, ranging all the way from lovely Greek Temples to equally lovely Colonial churches of our own country. Any good encyclopedia will furnish you with illustrations which you can follow. Who knows? Perhaps you will develop talent that will lead to your becoming an architect later on in life.

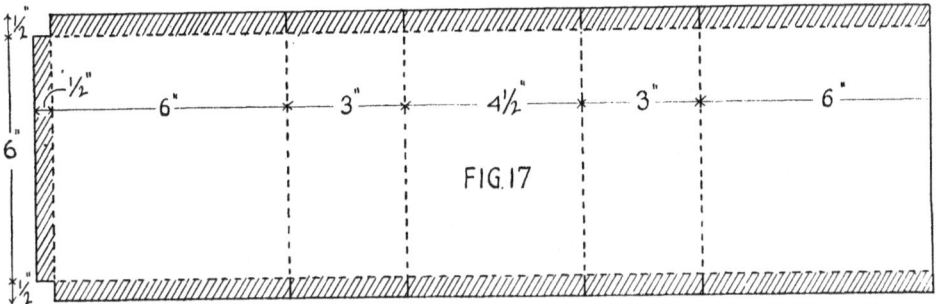

FIG. 17

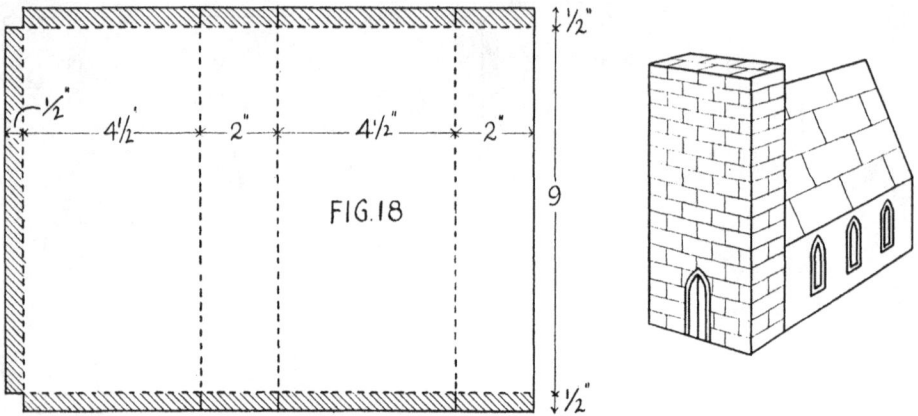

FIG. 18

How to make an Airplane Hangar or Garage

FIRST draw a shape to represent the end view of the building—and these directions by the way will apply to practically any building of simple construction you would like to build. This method gives you a piece of cardboard which includes in one piece, the floor, side walls and roof. The method followed in making the bird house gives you in one piece the side walls and end walls. That is the method to follow when you want eaves and gables. In building houses you can easily figure out how to add bay windows, chimneys, porches and so on, once you get the knack of LePage's Toy-Craft. The larger the building the heavier the cardboard.

To go back to the shape you are to draw for the garage. This will look something like Fig. 19. You can make the dimensions as large as you please. Cut out this shape. Measure each of the edges like, A B, B C, C D, D E and E A. Now refer to Fig. 17 under building a church. There you have certain dimensions beginning from left to right, ½″, 6″, etc. In the same way for your garage, beginning at the left with ½″ for a flange, mark off to the right the lengths of the lines A B, B C, C D, D E and E A on Fig. 19. Refer

again to Fig. 17. The width of the long strip is 6″. Decide how long you want your garage to be inside. This length should correspond to the line on Fig. 17 which in that case is 6″. Allow a ½″ flange in addition to this length, top and bottom. See Fig. 20. Score and fold, lepaging flange at extreme left inside edge at extreme right. Now lepage shape like Fig. 19 to flanges at one open end of the garage.

Cut a piece of cardboard the exact size and shape of the triangle formed by the lines A B, B C and C A, Fig. 19. Lepage this to the flanges of the gable at the front end of the garage. Now cut a piece of cardboard the exact size and shape indicated by the lines A C, C D, D E and E A. See Fig. 21. Cut in two along line F G. Score along dotted lines as indicated. Lepage sections to left and right of scored lines to the flanges still remaining at the front of the garage. This gives you wide swinging doors. Cut away any parts of the flanges still unused.

A hangar or garage of this kind can be made large enough to house your airplane or your motor cars and trucks, which you will make later on according to directions given on later pages of this book.

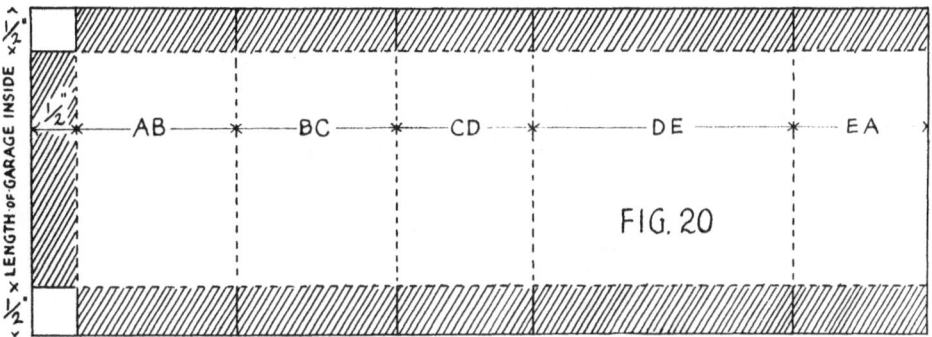

FIG. 20

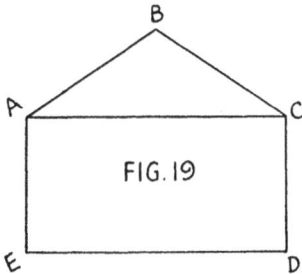

FIG. 19

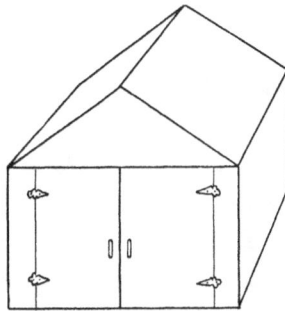

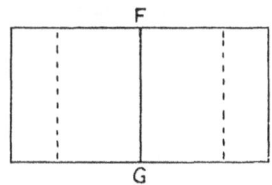

FIG. 21

How to make a Dutch Windmill

For the base of the windmill cut a piece of cardboard 6" square. Cut and score as shown in Fig. 22. Cut and score the corner pieces and lepage each inside the edge it comes next to when the long scored lines are folded.

Cut four pieces of cardboard, following Fig. 23. Flanges are left at top and bottom and along one side. Cover each of the side flanges with LePage's and fasten the four pieces to form the lower pyramid of the windmill. Fold bottom flanges underneath and lepage to center of base.

Now make a cap to cover this pyramid, following Fig. 22, except that this time your main dimensions instead of being 5" are 3", and your flange 1/4" instead of 1/2". Lepage this on top of the pyramid.

Cut a strip of cardboard 8 1/2" x 4" Score 1/2" flange at left. Score 1/2" flange at top and bottom, and cut the top and bottom flanges into saw teeth. Cut a hole where the black spot is about as large as a pencil is around, for the wing shaft. Bend the strip around to form a cylinder, lepaging the flange at the left to the inside of the right hand edge. Trace outline of one end and cut out circle of cardboard so traced. Keep this circle. Lepage one set of saw tooth flanges to the top of the platform which you lepaged on the pyramid, taking care that the hole of the wing shaft is above the center of one of the sides of the pyramid.

You now need a piece of round soft wood, 4" long and about half the size of a pencil. To one end of this shaft attach the wings by means of a pin. The wings are cut from a piece of cardboard 5 3/4" square, following Fig. 25 accurately. The circle at the center is traced round a penny, as are also the other curves shown. Insert the wing shaft through the wing shaft hole and fasten to the opposite wall of the cyl-

FIG 22

FIG. 26

FIG 24

FIG. 23

FIG. 25

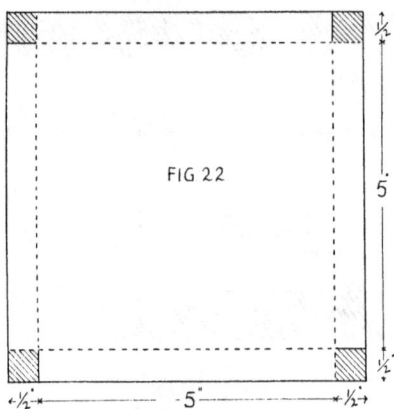

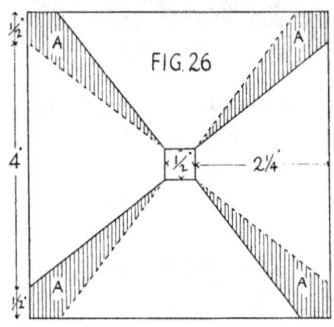

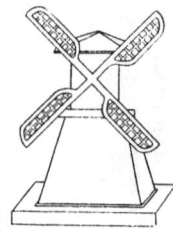

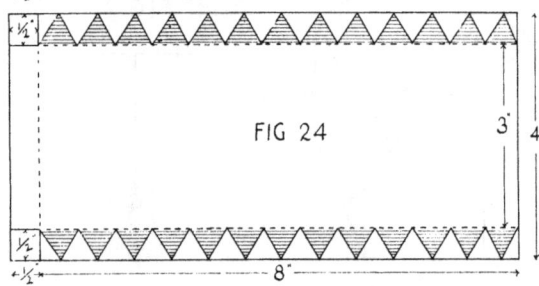

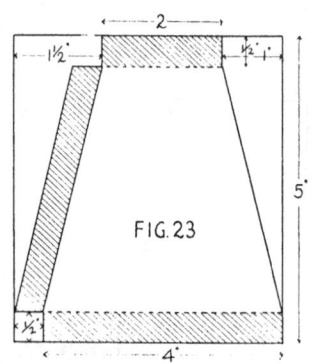

indrical part of the mill with another pin pushed through from outside. Now lepage the circle of cardboard which you made as directed above, to the top of the cylinder.

Now cut out the top, following Fig. 26. Trim off edges of flanges A flush to edge of roof and lepage together. Where edges touch top of cylinder put a drop of Lepage's and fasten roof in place.

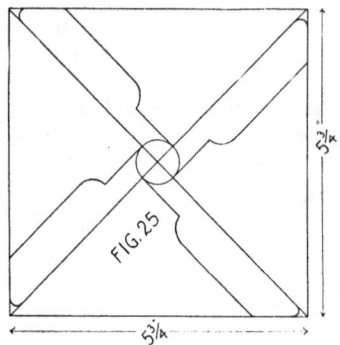

How to make a Playground Chute

CUT a piece of cardboard 12″ x 3″ as in Fig. 27. Score ½″ margin on each long side for sides of chute. At one end score crosswise each ¼″ for 2½″. Saw tooth the sides as shown. Cut out two strips like Fig. 28, which is shown about one-third size. Lepage these to the saw tooth section of the chute.

To make ladder cut two pieces of cardboard ½″ wide and 7″ long on one side and 6⅞″ long on the other. See Fig. 29.

Cut eleven steps like Fig. 30 and lepage in place between side members. Lepage top ends of side members of slide inside top of side members of ladder. Notice finished toy. Now construct and lepage in place support for lower end of slide, following Fig. 31.

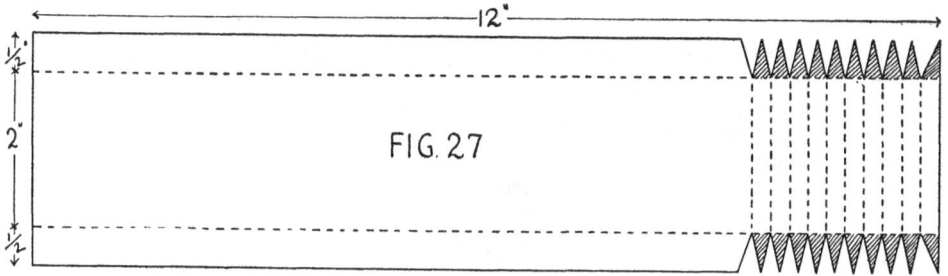

FIG. 27

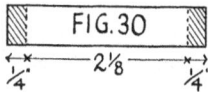

FIG. 30

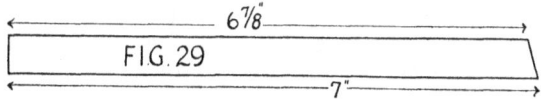

FIG. 29

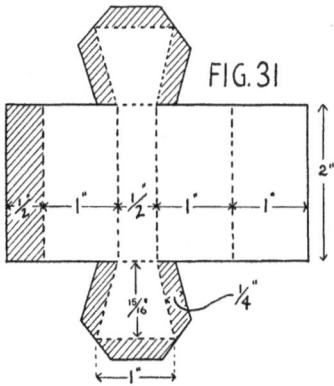

FIG. 31

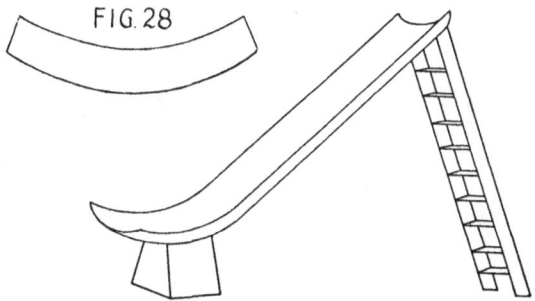

FIG. 28

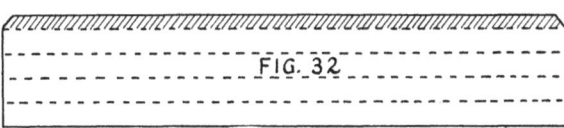

FIG. 32

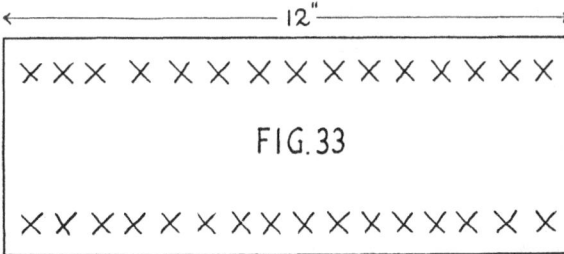

FIG. 33

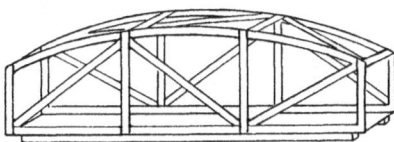

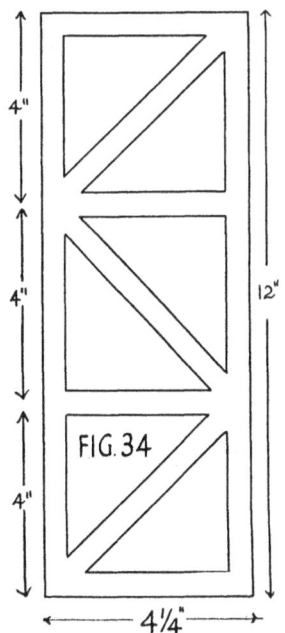

FIG. 34

How to make a Steel Bridge

YOU can easily make a bridge strong enough to run your toy train over. For the roadbed cut a strip of cardboard 12″ x 4¼″, see Fig. 33. Reinforce this underneath by lepaging girders, made according to Fig. 32, along paths indicated by crosses. Cut out a shape for the top member like that shown in Fig. 34. Now cut strips for the upright members ½″ wide. Fasten to the edges of the roadbed with flanges ½″ square. Allow ½″ flange on the upper end of each. Cut the four end uprights shorter than the four center uprights and lepage flanges to under side of top member. Lepage strips cornerwise on the side members as shown in the finished bridge. You can build a bridge any size, building it up from triangles, the only rigid geometrical figure.

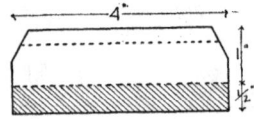

FIG. 37

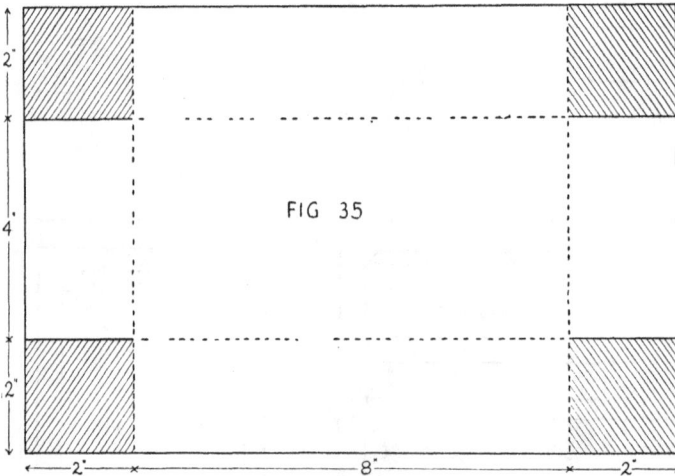

FIG 35

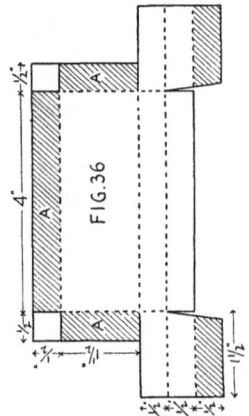

FIG. 36

How to make a Wagon

THE body of the wagon is made following Fig. 35, from a piece of cardboard 12″ x 8″. The seat is made according to Fig. 36. Flanges A, A, A fold down and are lepaged inside and at one end of the top of the body of the wagon. Cut a footrest, following Fig. 37, and lepage flange beneath front of wagon at the same end as the seat. Score and bend up front of footrest.

The supports which hold the axle are made exactly as you made the upright support of the bird house, see Fig. 13, except that the measurement of 8½″ becomes 4″. In the support which you use for the rear wheels, make the axle hole above the center of the ends. In the other support make the axle hole below the center. This will provide for making the rear wheels larger than the front wheels. The holes should be about the size of a pencil. Lepage these axle supports 1″ from the front and 1¾″ from the rear of the under side of the wagon.

The wheels themselves are made with compasses. For the rear wheels use a radius of 1½″. For the front wheels use a radius of 1¼″. This is figuring that the axle hole for the rear wheels is ¼″ below the wagon body, and that the axle hole for the front wheels is ¾″ below the wagon body. Draw another circle inside the outside rim of each wheel, leaving ¼″ between. Draw a circle for the hub of ¼″ radius. Mark out the spokes and cut out the parts between. Make holes through the hubs the size of a pencil. Make tubes of

cardboard which will just slip through these holes. Let these tubes be ½″ long and lepage each wheel securely in the center of one of them. Now prepare two straight round sticks of wood each 5½″ long, that fit the tubes loosely and at the same time fit the holes in the axle supports snugly. Run these axles through from side to side, slip a wheel on each projecting end. To prevent the wheels from coming off, lepage circles of cardboard ¼″ in diameter over the ends of the axles. Attach strips of cardboard underneath the front end for shafts. Paint red or blue. Letter in gold and paint gold flashes on the spokes.

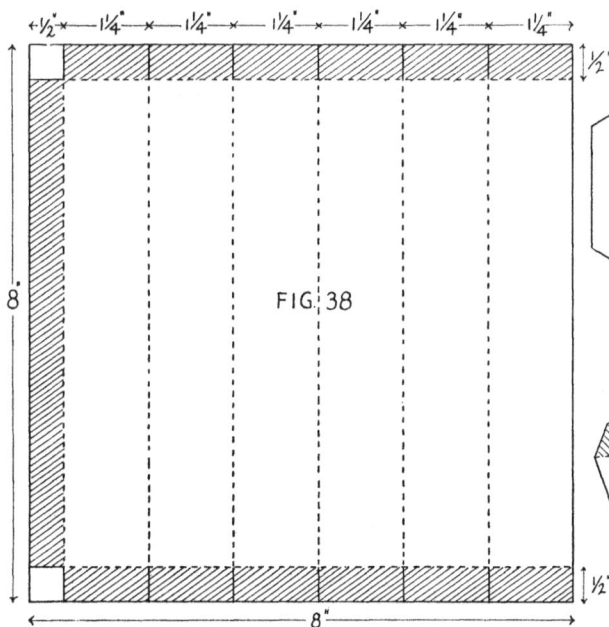

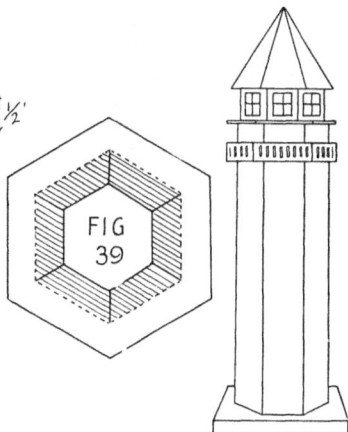

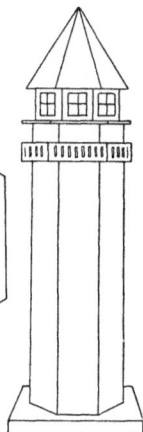

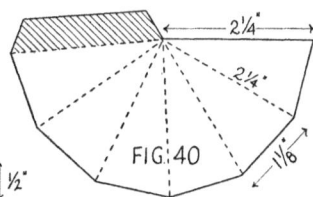

FIG 38

FIG 39

FIG 40

How to make a Lighthouse

THE base on which the hexagonal column of the lighthouse rests is made exactly as you made the base for the Dutch Windmill, see Fig. 22, except that instead of a piece of cardboard 6″ square, you start with one 4″ square. To make the hexagonal shaft you will

need a piece of cardboard 8″ square. Mark this as shown in Fig. 38. Fold up and lepage flange at left to inside of edge at right. Lepage flanges at one open end to center of base. Trace the outline of the other hexagonal end on a piece of cardboard. Draw a second hexagon outside this first one, leaving $\frac{1}{2}''$ between them. Draw a third hexagon inside the first one, leaving $\frac{1}{2}''$ between them. See Fig. 39. Cut as indicated. The center entirely cuts out. The flanges bend down and you slip this over the top of the hexagonal column and lepage in place 1" below the top to form the observation platform.

Again trace around the top of the column on a piece of cardboard and cut out a hexagon $\frac{1}{4}''$ larger all around than the top of the column. Bend in the flanges at the top of the column and lepage this hexagon to them.

Now cut out the section which forms the chamber in which the light is located. This is made like Fig. 38 except that the dimensions are changed. The flanges remain $\frac{1}{2}''$ wide. The

sides $1\frac{1}{4}''$ wide become 1" wide. The height is only 2" instead of 8". Lepage this in place. Now cut the roof, following Fig. 40. Fold into shape and lepage. Then spread LePage's along the top edges of the lantern room and place the roof on it and let dry. The fence around the observation platform is merely a strip of cardboard long enough to go all around the platform, with a flange at the bottom for lepaging to the platform, and holes cut in it to give it the appearance of an iron railing supported by iron rods.

If you are a good electrician, you can rig a light in the lantern room. To let it shine through, cut out the windows and cover with tissue paper. If you plan on this, better do it before you lepage the lantern room in place.

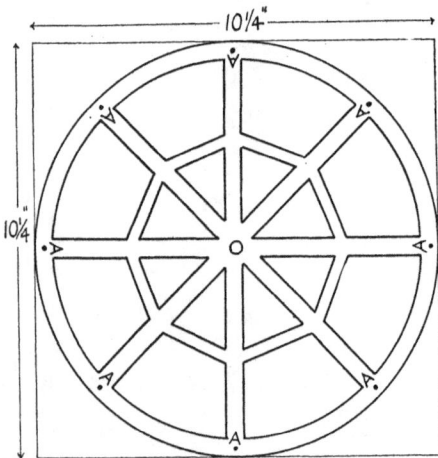

FIG. 41

FIG. 42

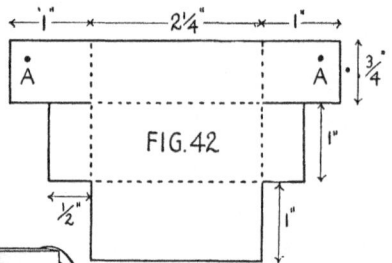

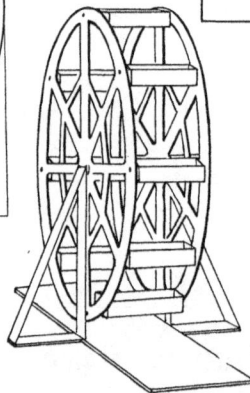

How to make a Ferris Wheel

THE base of this wonder of the amusement park is made as you made the base of the Dutch windmill. (See Fig. 22) the measurements being

changed as follows: The size over all including flanges, is $13\frac{1}{2}''$ x 6". The flanges are $\frac{1}{2}''$ all around. In the center of each long side, cut out $\frac{1}{2}''$ length from the flange. Through the holes left in the flanges a crosswise supporting beam is to be laid beneath the platform. Make this beam as you made the upright support of the bird house. See Fig. 13. The length of cardboard for making this beam is 14¼" which allows for ¼" flanges at the ends. The four sides are each ½" wide instead of 1" wide as in Fig. 13. Cut out this beam and lepage together. Then lepage it to the under side of the platform so that 4⅜" stick out on each side. Where the flanges on the long sides of the platform meet this beam, make the joints secure with hinges underneath and inside.

Now make the two beams that form the upright supports for the wheel. These beams are also made as you made the support for the bird house. See Fig. 13. The width of each side is ½". That is, you start with a piece of cardboard 2½" x 8". Flanges are left at one end only this time. On the other end, cut half circles on opposite sides, large enough for a pencil to rest in loosely. These grooved ends are the tops of the uprights. Lepage the bottom ends of the uprights to the platform on opposite edges just above where the cross beam which supports the platform comes through the sides of the platform, being sure that the grooves in the tops of the uprights are parallel to the ends of the platform. To give these uprights greater security, lepage ½" wide strips of cardboard from its sides to the edges of the platform and to the end of the crossbeam. There are 6 of these supports; 3 to each upright.

Now cut out two wheels from heavy cardboard, following Fig. 41. Each wheel is made from a piece of cardboard 10¼" square. The spokes are ½" wide. The hub is as large as a half dollar, and the axle hole is as large around as a pencil. Use compasses to describe the circumference of the wheel. To find the center of the square, draw diagonals from corner to corner. Where they cross is the center. Use a radius equal to the distance from the center of the square to the center of any side. The dots at points marked A are pinholes where the carriages are to hang. There are eight carriages, each made like Fig. 42. Again the dots at points A, A represent pinholes that will correspond with the pinholes on the wheels. Cut the axle, a piece of wood as large round as a pencil and 7½" long.

Now mount the two wheels on the axle. Then mount the carriages to the wheels by means of pins through corresponding pinholes. To keep the wheels permanently at the same distance apart, cut 8 strips of cardboard ½" wide and 3½" long. Make a flange at each end ½" long. Lepage these between the wheels on the main spokes half way from the circumference to the center.

How to make a Mill and Water Wheel

THE base is a piece of heavy cardboard 11½" x 8". On one end erect the mill house, which is made as you made the garage. See Fig. 19. Your strip of cardboard is 8" wide. On this mark off, beginning at the left, ½" for a flange; 8" for the first side of the house; 4" for the first slant of the roof; 4" for the second slant of the roof; 8" for the other side of the house; ½" for a flange. Score and bend and lepage flanges to base so that house sits at one end of the base.

Now cut a hole large enough for a pencil to slip through in each of the two side walls of the house, 3½" from the floor and 2¼" from the end of the house. You will need a stick of wood as large around as a pencil and 12" long. Thrust this through the two holes. Lepage a small circle of cardboard on the end which sticks out of the house on

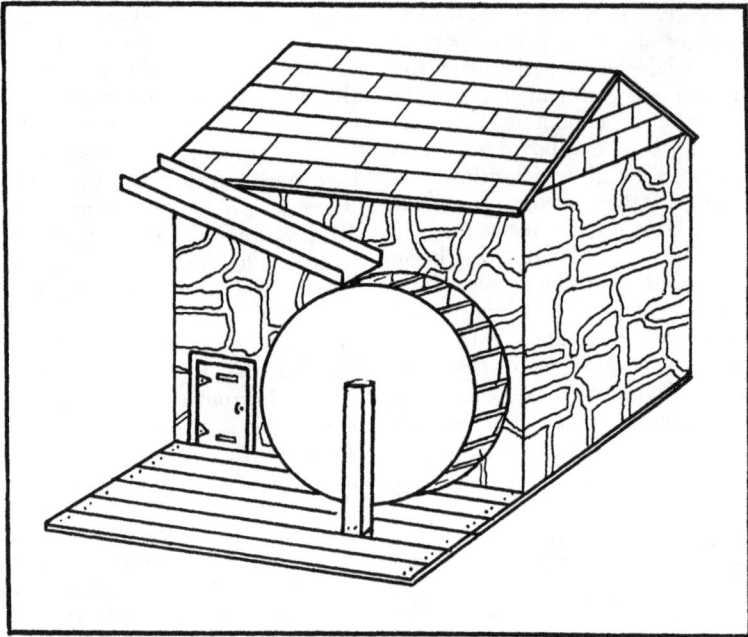

the side opposite the platform, where the mill wheel is to stand. Now trace the outlines of the open ends of the house on cardboard. Add ½" flange all around to these shapes and lepage to the open ends of the house.

Now make the wheel. Cut out two circles of cardboard 3" in radius. Cut a hole in the center of each large enough for the shaft to slip through. Cut a strip of cardboard 3" wide and 13" long. Leave ½" flange at one end and ½" flange at both sides. The side flanges are to be cut saw tooth, as this strip is to be curved to form the drum of the wheel. On each of the circles you cut out, draw circles of 2" radius from the same center. The circumference of these circles of 2" radius is the line along which you

lepage the saw tooth flanges of the drum.

Now cut 16 pieces 3" long and ⅞" wide, leaving ½" flanges at each end. Lepage these in place on the wheel to form the troughs or buckets into which the water runs. Slip this completed wheel onto the wooden shaft.

To support the end of the shaft, make an upright column, as you made the upright support for the bird house. See Fig. 13. Each side is ¾" wide and the height of the finished column is 5". Cut a hole in one side for the shaft of wood to slip into. Slip it in and lepage the base of the column to the platform. Lepage a water trough to the side of the mill as shown in the illustration.

How to make a War Tank

FIRST cut out a piece of cardboard, following the dimensions and scoring as shown in Fig. 43. This forms in one piece, the top, ends and bottom of the tank. Fig. 44 shows the sides, of

which you will need two. Follow dimensions carefully. The curves are obtained by tracing around a nickel. The flange is saw toothed around the curves as shown. When you have the first

FIG. 43

FIG. 44

FIG. 45

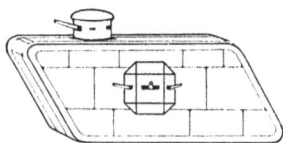

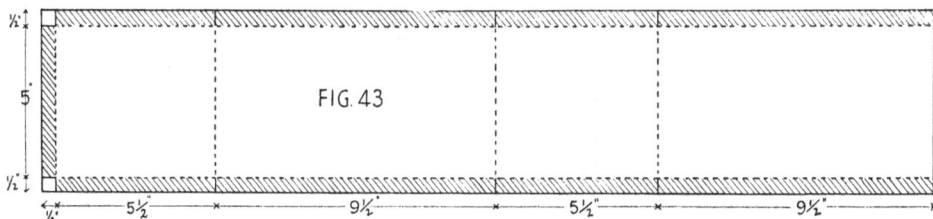

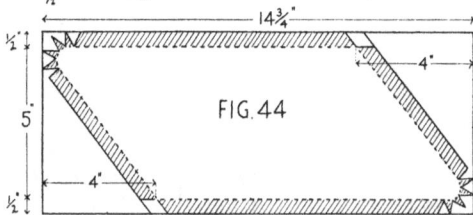

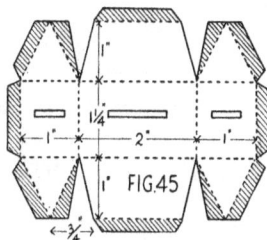

side made lay it down with the flanges bent upward. Now on the shape you made from Fig. 43, bend in the flanges around one of the open sides, cover them with LePage's and lepage to the side made from Fig. 44. The edges of the side will project ½" all around the shape, Fig. 43. Attach the other side in the same way.

Now cut 2 strips of cardboard each 1" wide and long enough to go all around the outline of the side. Lepage this in place on the flange which you left on the side. These form the cater-pillar tread. The two side turrets are made according to Fig. 45. Follow this carefully for measurements and flanges. Make two of them. Cut slots for guns. Fold and lepage into shape, and lepage in place on the tank as shown in the finished drawing.

The roof turret needs first a plat-form, made exactly as you made the ground platform for the windmill. See Fig. 22. The finished platform is 3" square. So first draw a 3" square on cardboard. Score it. Draw a 3½" square evenly all around it. Score it. Draw a 4" square evenly all around the second one and cut out. Cut out the corner pieces; fold and lepage in place on the roof of the tank. The gun cham-ber in this turret is made of a strip of cardboard, 8½" x 2" with ½" left at one end for a flange, and ½" left at each side for a flange. Score crosswise beginning at left ½", 1", 2", 3", 4", 5", 6", 7". Fold and lepage into shape. Trace the outline of this octagonal opening on a piece of cardboard. Le-page flanges of one open side to the platform which you just made. Then add ⅛" to octagon just made and lepage this in place on the top of the octagonal gun chamber.

How to make a Motor Truck

FIRST, make the frame as follows: Cut a strip of cardboard 24" x 1¾". Score a flange ½" wide on each long side. Then starting at one end of the

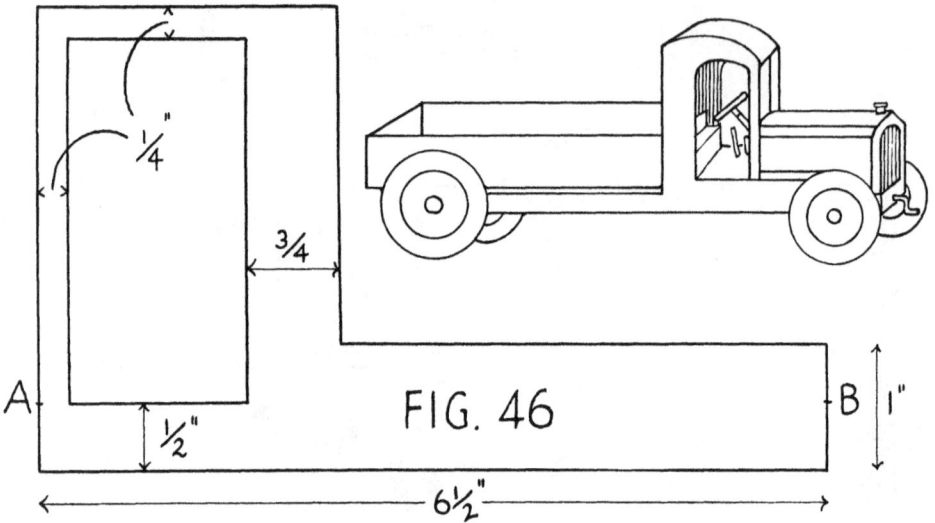

FIG. 46

strip mark off and score ½" from the end; 8" from that point; 3¾" from that point; 8" from that point, and 3¾" from that point. Cut the side flanges where you score across; fold around and lepage into shape. Make 4 axle holes size of a pencil in the side members of this frame; close to the ends in each case; close to the top for the rear wheels; close to the bottom for the front wheels. Cut two axles of wood, one 7" long and one 5½" long, each as large around as a pencil.

Cut a piece of cardboard 8" x 3¾" and lepage this to the flanges on the top side of the frame. Then make the side pieces, of which you will need two like Fig. 46. Lepage these to the outside of the side members of the frame so that the points A and B are at the level of the top of the frame, and the point B at the extreme rear end of the frame.

To make the seat you need a piece of cardboard 4¾" x 3½". Score ½" flange along both of the long edges and ½" flange along one of the shorter edges. Parallel with the shorter edges score across at ½" from one end; ¾" from the first scoring; ¾" from the second scoring and at ¾" from the third

scoring. Fold into shape and lepage into place between uprights of the top. For the canopy cut a strip of cardboard 8½" x 4¾" leaving ½" flange on the short sides. Score across 2½" from one end; fold and lepage in place. Make a steering wheel as you made the wheels of the wagon. See description under "How to make a Wagon." The road wheels are all made alike, except for the difference in size. The radius of each rear wheel is 1½" and its tread is 1" wide. The radius of each front wheel is 1⅛" and its tread is ¼" wide. To make one of the rear wheels, with compasses and a radius of 1½" mark out and cut out two circles of cardboard. Punch a hole in the center of each circle, as large as the axle. Cut a strip of cardboard 2" wide and 9⅜" long. Score a ½" flange at one end and along each side. Cut the side flanges saw tooth. Bend around and lepage to form the rim or tread of the wheel. Lepage the saw tooth flanges on one side to the circumference of one of the circles. Then lepage the other circle on and the wheel is finished.

To make the hood, cut a strip of cardboard 7" long x 4" wide. Score ½" flange all around and cut out the corners. Score crosswise into 4 equal divisions of $1\frac{1}{2}$" each, not counting the end flanges.

Trace the outline of the open ends on cardboard. Lepage one to the flanges in front and one to the flanges in rear.

Along the one on the rear cut off $\frac{1}{2}$" from the bottom. Now lepage this hood in position, the side flanges coming down $\frac{1}{2}$" over the outside of the side members of the frame and back as far as the front uprights that support the canopy.

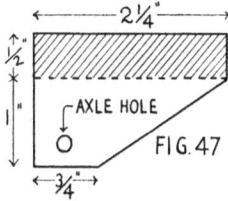

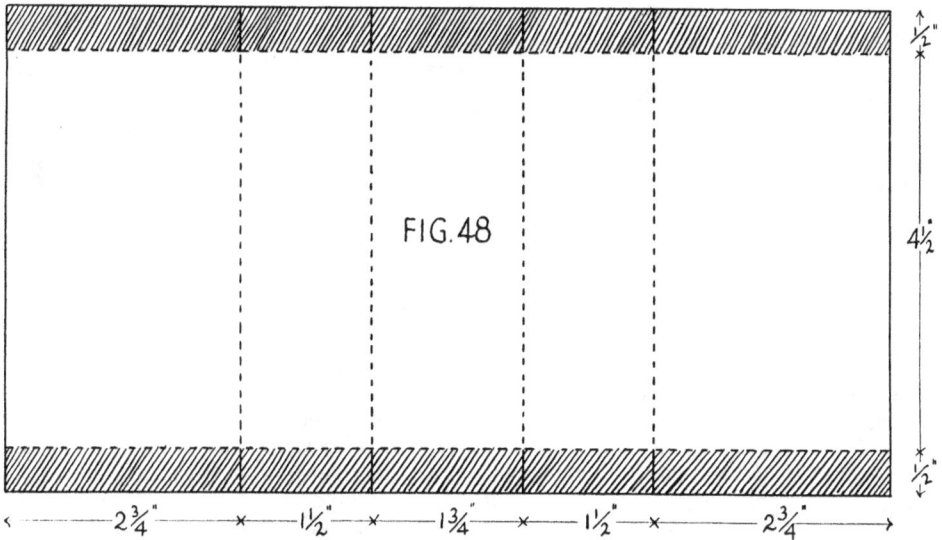

FIG. 47

FIG. 48

How to make a Tractor

FIRST make the frame. Cut a strip of cardboard $1\frac{3}{4}$" wide by $23\frac{1}{2}$" long. Score a $\frac{1}{2}$" flange across one end and along both sides. Then beginning at the end where the flange is, score across, at a point $8\frac{1}{4}$" from the flange; score across $3\frac{1}{4}$" from this point; $8\frac{1}{4}$" again. Cut side flanges at scoring. Fold into shape of frame and lepage together. Lepage an $8\frac{1}{4}$" x $3\frac{1}{4}$" piece of cardboard on top for the floor.

Two supports for the front axle are needed. See Fig. 47. The flange should not be scored in this particular case.

It is used to lepage the supports to the front ends of the side members of the frame so that the broken line runs even with the lower edge of the side of the frame.

To build the hood, follow Fig. 48. Fold and lepage extreme left and right ends to outside of front end of side members of frame so that the edges run even with the lower edges of the side members. Trace the open front and rear ends on cardboard. Cut out the shapes and lepage in place. The wheels are made in the same way as for the motor truck, except that you can cut out holes to leave spokes if you wish. The radius of the rear wheels is $2\frac{1}{4}''$ and the tread 1". The radius of the front wheels is $1\frac{1}{4}''$ and the tread is $\frac{1}{2}''$.

The rear axle is $6\frac{1}{2}''$ long and the front one $4\frac{3}{4}''$. Thrust another stick made like an axle into the rear end of the hood and lepage a circle of cardboard on the end for a steering wheel. And you are ready to undertake some modern farming.

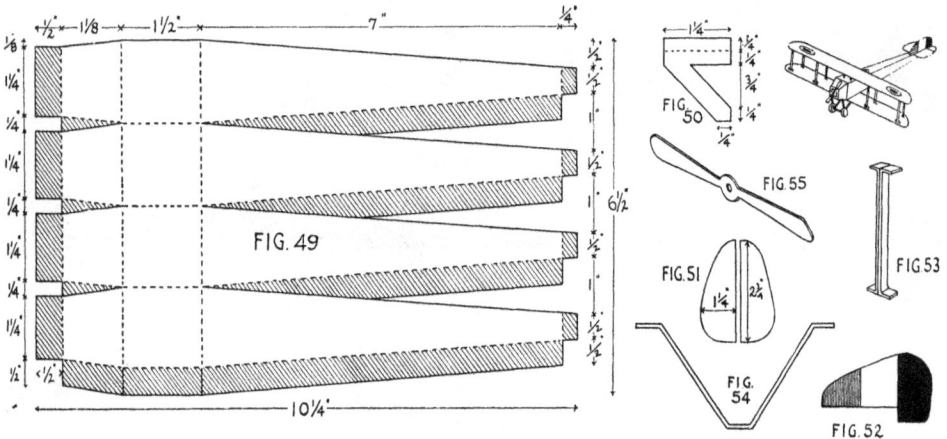

FIG. 49

FIG. 50

FIG. 55

FIG. 51

FIG 53

FIG. 54

FIG. 52

How to make an Airplane

TO MAKE the body of the airplane, follow Fig. 49. Follow dimensions and scoring very carefully. Fold and lepage into shape. Cut a piece of cardboard $\frac{1}{2}''$ square and lepage to flanges at rear end. Cut a piece of cardboard $1\frac{1}{4}''$ square and lepage to flanges of the front end. To make the skid on which the tail rests when the plane is on the ground, cut out two shapes like Fig. 50. Lepage them together up to the dotted line. Score on this line and fold the 2 halves away from each other. Lepage the surface so formed to the underside of the tail $\frac{1}{2}''$ from the end. The side tail pieces are made like Fig. 51. Each half is $1\frac{1}{4}''$ wide in its widest part and $2\frac{3}{4}''$ long. Lepage these shapes to the top of the tail with $1\frac{1}{8}''$ reaching beyond the end. Top tail piece is made like Fig. 52. It is $2\frac{1}{4}''$ tall and $2\frac{3}{4}''$ long. Lepage this on top of the tail, projecting beyond the end $1\frac{1}{8}''$. Use hinges of thin paper for this lepaging.

The top wing is $12\frac{3}{4}''$ x $2\frac{1}{4}''$. The lower wing is $10\frac{1}{4}''$ x $1\frac{1}{2}''$. Lepage the lower wing directly to the underside of the square section of the body and so that $4\frac{1}{4}''$ project on each side. Now cut the struts. See Fig. 53. Each of these is made of 2 strips of cardboard $\frac{1}{4}''$ wide and 3 inches long. Score off $\frac{1}{2}''$ at each end of each strip. Bend flanges at right angles and lepage the two strips together back to back. You will need 8 of these and also 4 others whose finished length is $\frac{1}{2}''$, that is, you would make them of strips $1\frac{1}{2}''$ x $\frac{1}{4}''$. Lepage one end of each of the four short ones on top of the body near the four corners. Lepage one end of each of the four long ones at the edges of the lower wing, and $1\frac{1}{2}''$ and $3\frac{1}{2}''$ away from the body. Then lepage the top wing to the top flanges of each of these 12 struts so that the front edge of the top wing is directly above the front edge of the lower wing, so that the top wing projects $5\frac{1}{2}''$ each side of the body.

Braces for the landing gear are made from strips of cardboard $\frac{1}{2}''$ wide. Score this strip $\frac{1}{2}''$ from the end; $2\frac{1}{4}''$ from the end; $2\frac{3}{4}''$ from the end; $4\frac{1}{4}''$ from the end; and finally cut off at a point $4\frac{3}{4}''$ from the end. Fold and lepage under the body, at the edge of the body, and just front and rear of the lower wing, longest leg to the front. Roll a strip of paper $3''$ wide tightly until it is as large around as a pencil. Lepage the edge in place. Cut out two circles of cardboard $1\frac{1}{2}''$ in diameter and lepage these to the ends of the roll of paper. This forms wheels and axle. Now lepage the feet of the landing gear to the top of the axle between the wheels. Cut a propeller $3\frac{1}{2}''$ long shaping the blades free hand. See Fig. 55. Attach to center of nose of plane with a pin.

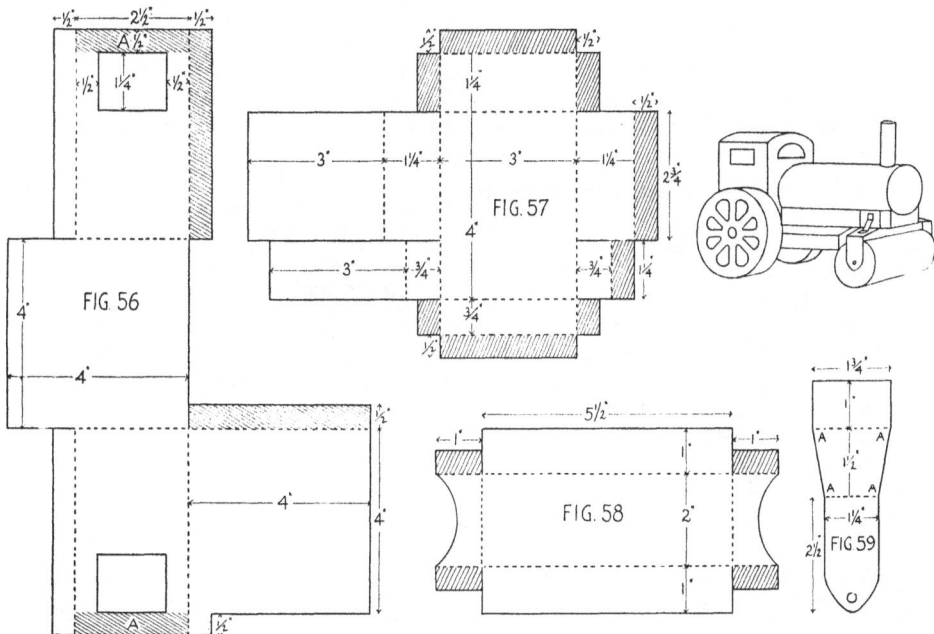

FIG. 56

FIG. 57

FIG. 58

FIG. 59

How to make a Road Roller

FIRST make the two rear wheels, following the method used in the tractor and auto truck wheels. Use a radius of $2\frac{1}{2}''$. Cut out the holes between the spokes and cut axle holes in the center as large round as a pencil. The width of the finished tread is $1\frac{3}{4}''$. That means the tread for each wheel will be a strip of cardboard $2\frac{3}{4}''$ wide and $16\frac{1}{4}''$ long. Leave $\frac{1}{2}''$ flange at one end and make saw tooth flanges $\frac{1}{2}''$ wide along each side. Lepage the saw tooth flanges to the inside edges of the circles and around the circumference. Make an axle of a strip of wood $9''$ long as large around as a pencil.

Now make the forward wheel. Cut a strip of cardboard $5\frac{1}{4}''$ wide and $9\frac{1}{2}''$ long. Leave $\frac{1}{2}''$ flange at one end and $\frac{1}{2}''$ flange, cut saw tooth, along each side. Score flanges and lepage end flange to inside edge of other end of strip. Cut 2 circles of cardboard, $1\frac{3}{8}''$ radius. Cut axle hole at center as before. Lepage these circles to saw tooth flanges.

Now make the cabin by following

Fig. 56. Cut out, score as indicated and lepage into shape. For the top cut a strip of cardboard 2½″ wide and 6″ long. Lepage in place between the flanges which you left in Fig. 56, A.A. This will be obvious to you when you reach this point.

Make the fire box following Fig. 57. Draw the diagram complete on cardboard and see that your solid and broken lines correspond exactly to Fig. 57 before scoring and cutting. This will make a box which has a jog cut out of the top of one end. Lepage this jog to the front of and underneath the cabin, and so that the larger part of the box will extend in front.

The boiler is a cylinder made from a strip of cardboard just as if it were a wheel with a very wide tread. Cut out two circles for the ends, each of radius 1¼″. Cut a strip 6¾″ wide and leave saw tooth flanges at each side ½″ wide, so that the finished width is 5¾″. The length of this strip is 8¼″ which includes a ½″ flange for joining the edges to form the cylinder. Now lepage the saw tooth edges to the circles as in making a wheel.

The cradle in which the boiler rests is a box with an open top and the ends rounded to fit the curve of the boiler. Follow Fig. 58. Lepage the top edges of this cradle and lay the boiler in it so that the rear of the boiler and rear end of the cradle are even up and down. Now lepage the cradle and boiler securely to the front of the cabin and top of fire box.

Make two forks like Fig. 59, to hold the front wheel on roller. Lepage one to each side of the cradle ½″ from the front end of the cradle. The section A.A.A.A. will be horizontal. The other two sections vertical. For strength, lepage a ½″ strip of cardboard from the center of the top of surface A.A.A.A. to the surface that is lepaged to the cradle. The axle holes are made the size of a pencil. Run the axle through the roller and insert between forks.

To support the rear axle lepage 2 short strips from the under side of the cabin to the rear end of the fire box. The smokestack is a cylinder of paper with saw tooth flanges at bottom to lepage to top of boiler.

How to make a Castle

FOR the base of the main part of the castle cut a piece of heavy cardboard 7″ square. Now make four square towers, following the method used for the support of the bird house. See Fig. 13. The finished height of each tower (without the cap which is made separately as described below) is 9½″. You will need a piece of cardboard 10½″ x 8½″. Score a ½″ flange along each 10½″ side and along one 8½″ side. Measuring away from the scoring on the 8½″ side, score off sections every 2″. Fold and lepage into shape. Lepage the flanges surrounding one open end of each tower to each of the four corners of the base. Join these towers by side walls of which there are four. Make each as follows: Cut four pieces of cardboard each 10″ x 4″. Score ½″ flange all around. Cut out corners. Lepage one end flange of each to the base between the towers and the 2 side flanges of each to the towers so that the outer surface of these side walls is set ½″ back from the edge of the base. To the upper flanges of these sidewalls cut strips of cardboard to fit and lepage in place, forming the roof.

Now make a cap for each tower like Fig. 60. Score, cut and lepage in shape. Then lepage to the flanges at the tops of the four towers. The lower side towers on two sides of this main part of the castle, which you have already made, are 7″ tall. They have three sides 2½″, 4″ and 2½″. Cut a strip of cardboard 7″ wide and beginning at one end

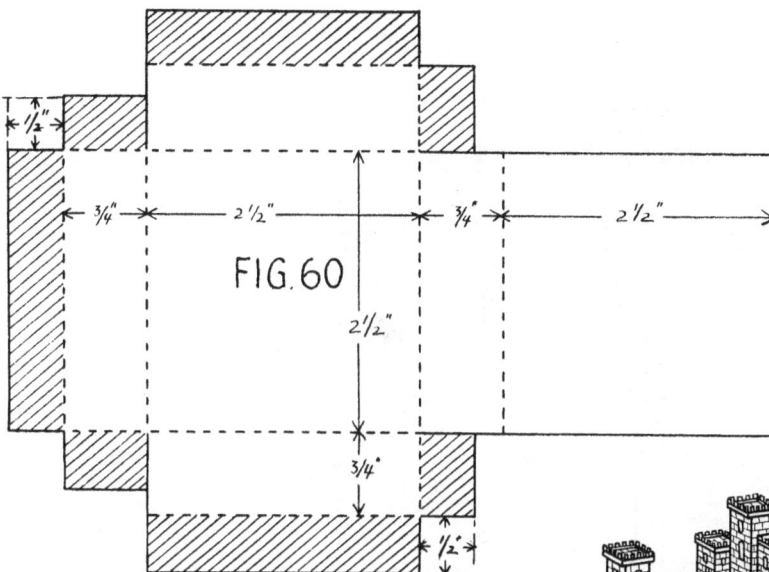

FIG. 60

score across making sections ½", 2½", 4", 2½" and ½". The ½" flanges at the ends lepage to the outer walls of the main towers and on opposite sides of the castle.

Now make 2 additional towers just as you made the 4 main towers. The height of these two is 7" and the width of each is 2½". Make caps for them and lepage in place. These 2 towers form the outer corners of the castle yard, and these towers are connected to the side towers of the castle by strips of cardboard forming a fence or wall 4½" high and 7" long. Now close the only remaining open side of the yard with a fence or wall of cardboard between the last two towers you made 7" long and 5" high.

Cut strips of cardboard ¾" wide and make square teeth ¼" deep along one edge. Lepage these around the tops of all the towers and walls.

How to make a Speed Boat

CUT the sides of the boat following Fig. 62. Lepage the bows together with a hinge. Cut the stern like Fig. 63 and lepage in place. Cut a bulkhead like Fig. 64 and lepage between the sides at the widest point, 5" from the bows. Cut the bottom like Fig. 65. Follow dimensions carefully. Snip out those long V-shaped pieces near the widest part. Lepage in place on the flanges surrounding the bottom. Cut another piece of cardboard like the forward part of the bottom and lepage to the flanges, along the top edges of the bows. Cut another piece of cardboard like the rear part of Fig. 65, leaving flanges at the sides which are ¾" wide at the forward end and taper to ¼"

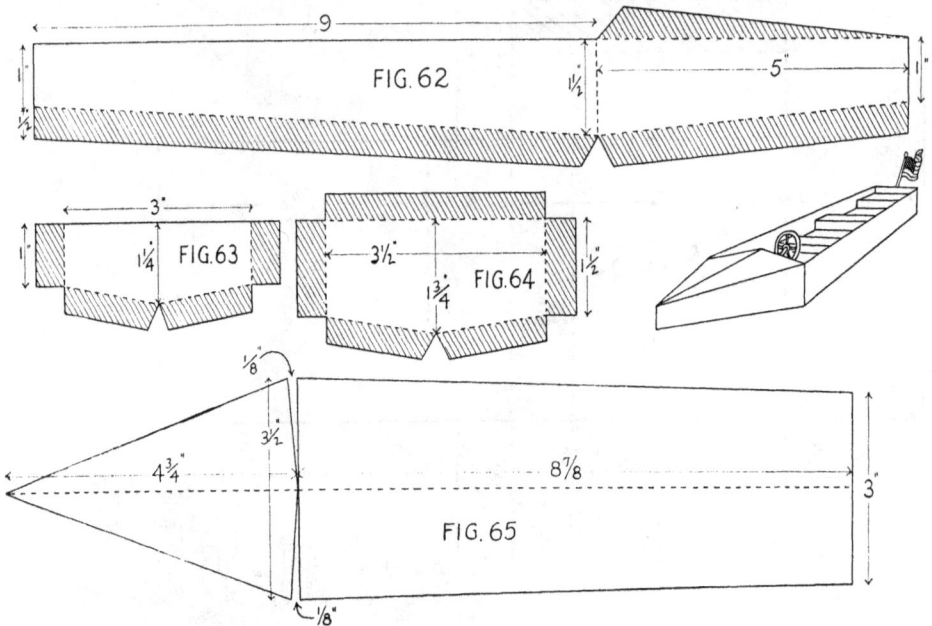

FIG. 62

FIG. 63

FIG. 64

FIG. 65

wide at the rear. Lepage this inside the boat to form the deck, the flanges giving it the proper height. Make seats and lepage in crosswise.

How to make Doll's Furniture

A SIMPLE chair can be made by following Figs. 66 and 67, cutting out, scoring, folding and lepaging together. Having made one chair, you can easily duplicate it, or you can make variations of it. You can make ladder backs and spindle backs, or copy any chair in the room. You can put rockers on them. You can make wing chairs. Instead of working out a complete diagram as in Figs. 66 and 67, you may find it easier to cut out the sides, back and seat separately and then put the parts together with hinges.

A table is made of a piece of cardboard 2″ x 2¾″ for the top with ¼″ flanges in addition all around, scored and bent down to show the thickness of the top of the table. Legs 2¼″ long may be lepaged to the corners underneath. Part way between the under side of the

top and the foot of the legs, you can put in another shelf 2⅛″ x 2¾″. See the illustration. Legs are made of strips of cardboard ½″ wide scored through the center lengthwise.

A Vanity Dresser as shown in the illustration is made in three parts. One part is a three panel screen. Each of the two tiny tables are made like Fig. 66 except that the measurements are changed. And then these are lepaged to the outside panels of the three panel screen. The screen is 4″ square divided into three panels of 1⅜″ each scalloped at the top. The top of each table is 1¼″ square and stands 1¾″ from the floor. Again, it may be easier to cut out each side and the top of the tables and then lepage them together with hinges.

A bureau is made like a box with one

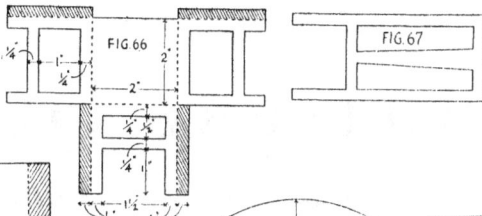

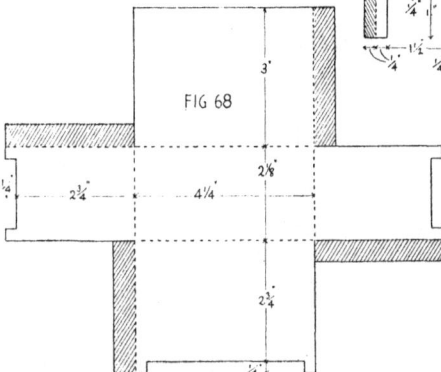

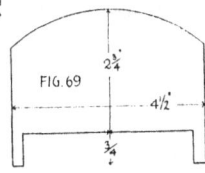

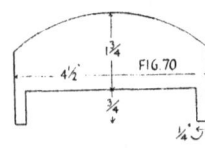

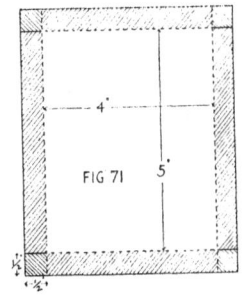

open end and then pieces cut away from the front and sides at the bottom, to form the legs at the corners. This may be cut out in one piece. See Fig. 68.

To make a bed, cut out a headboard and footboard like Fig. 69 and Fig. 70, and round off the corners. Cut the bed like Fig. 71, with ½" flanges all around. Fold and lepage into shape, and then lepage between the headboard and footboard just above the tops of the legs.

Decorate with cretonne if you wish.

LEPAGE'S GLUE
is a great Mender

IN THE fascination of making toys with LePage's Glue do not forget that LePage's is a wonderful mender of broken things. You can make yourself very handy around the home as the family repairman. There are almost as many occasions for using LePage's Glue for mending as there are drops of glue in a LePage's tube. Many people have told us that they would find it very difficult to keep house without it. It proves useful in many unexpected ways. Just having a tube handy in the house is enough to suggest its use whenever anything breaks.

Many a doll's broken leg or arm or even neck has been easily and skilfully mended with LePage's. Many a broken toy has been made as good as new again.

Often with the help of LePage's and at practically no cost, you can mend and restore to use a broken article that otherwise would cause an expense either of having it repaired in a shop or of buying a new one.

You can stiffen the end of a shoe lace if the metal tip pulls off and save fussing with the frayed end and save the cost of a new pair. You can quickly refasten handles that pull off of umbrellas, whisk brooms, powder puffs, nail files, etc. You can refasten loose rungs in chairs, and mend torn bookbindings.

A loose tile in the bathroom or in the hearth of a fireplace may be refastened with LePage's instead of paying a mason to do it.

You can save quite a bit of money for your father and mother if you keep your eyes open for chances to mend with LePage's. And perhaps they will gladly give you a modest sum for repairs which would cost considerably more if a workman were hired to make them.

What do you think of
Lepage's Toy-Craft?

After you have made a few of the toys described in this book, the Editor will be very glad to receive a letter from you, if you care to write one, telling us how you like LePage's Craft. We will consider it a very special favor if you do so. Please address: Editor's Office, LePage's Craft League, Gloucester, Mass.

www.ingramcontent.com/pod-product-compliance
Lightning Source LLC
Chambersburg PA
CBHW031618040426
42452CB00006B/584